PAST 3AM

TARYN KISAALITA

— Taryn . K

Thanks for reading !

Taryn . K

for the ones

that loved me

before i did

~ My mother, Josephine

& My brother, Tygris

Library of Congress Control Number:		2021909965
ISBN:	Hardcover	978-1-5434-9293-4
	Softcover	978-1-5434-9292-7
	eBook	978-1-5434-9291-0

Print information available on the last page.

Rev. date: 05/12/2021

To order additional copies of this book, contact:
Xlibris
UK TFN: 0800 0148620 (Toll Free inside the UK)
UK Local: 02036 956328 (+44 20 3695 6328 from outside the UK)
www.Xlibrispublishing.co.uk
Orders@Xlibrispublishing.co.uk
786484

CONTENTS

CHAPTER 1

IT'S OKAY

you were so worried
that i would fail
so now i fear
even trying at all

why even wake up
now that i don't want to breathe
why exhibit a smile
when it contradicts all that i feel

i mistook
love for admiration
so when it came to the end
i hurt myself for nothing

what i hate
about growing up
is that
one day you wake up
and the ones you're meant to love
are the ones
you resent the most

i thought
you were my safety net
but you were the claws
pulling me down
further into your manipulative grasp

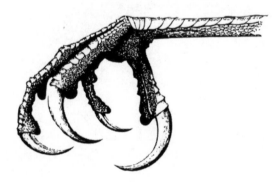

i never wanted to lose you
so i neglected the burns
you sparked with your
hateful fires

i'm one with perfect vision
that acts like they
cannot see

it wasn't your absence
that hurt
it was your
pointless return

i don't understand
how people say they're sorry
but can still stand
to hurt you
in a different way

sometimes i wish
that i were in
a video game
so at least
i'd have more lives
to start again

my stomach curls
Encircled by a myriad
of friends

even though
there's so many to go around
why do i always feel
like i don't belong

they make a completed outfit
but i'm just
the accessory
that rusts in the box

and as time goes on
the latch
that once opened
can never
be opened again

the person
i look up to
changed who i was

so if you ask me
who i am
all i could say
would be
my name

i am not
eager for attention
but i feel
like i'm the only one
putting in effort
when i thought
that we had
to meet halfway

what you did
hurt me
what you didn't do
ended me

sometimes
i hate starting again
because
it means having to look
back at the mistakes
that i continuously
regret

you see my
curly hair out of
the braids enclosed
in its core
and think
wow is it real
i've never seen this
before

the sun
embraces my skin
in ways you didn't
before
but wait
i'm a shade darker
now no one wants me
anymore

light is perfection
but dark means
rejection
it's just my skin
complexion
but you make it feel
like an unfortunate
infection

our curves and
tender lips
on the ends
of your fingertips
the hourglass body
you desire
was laughable for me
when i was young and
under pressure

the standards
society constructed
were we not the
foundation?
and yet i'll
still get ranked most
despicable
by the rest of the
nation

- why do you despise **me**

fooling everyone
is an easy task
but fooling myself
is a different
kind of ask

the sad part is
i still wait
for you to come back

and what's even sadder
is that
i would let you

i always blamed you
for not getting
what i wanted

but it was easier
than blaming myself
for being too afraid

why do i feel so
pushed away

when i was never
brought close
in the first place

your words
shackle me in my tomb
but my lack
of courage
makes the key
harder to find

i walked freely
into the cave
with you
as my light

but when you left
so suddenly
i couldn't
find my way out

why was i looking
for what was
already gone

when you walked into my life
you never really left
i still see
your petrifying shadow
lingering in the doorway

like a thorn
waiting to prick me
if i just got
a little bit closer

blood
sweat and
tears

for me it's
love
regret and
fears

happiness used to
live rent free
in the depths of my soul
but ever since
it left my temple
only a negative stream
has inhabited
what's left
of my worn out
place

father
a word i struggle so greatly
to say
my DNA will say
he's my father indeed
but a father
isn't what he's been to me

do fathers
remain a mystery
until they feel
like waltzing in so
effortlessly

i give my heart
my trust
my patience
but what do i get
at the end of the story
nothing but
agony
saved especially
for me

i'm the *therapist* friend
when their world starts to erode
i help them build it again

but when my world
fades away
they silently observe
like they never cared

because
they never did

the top of a skyscraper
seems like the best place
to be

from so far up
you don't have to see
the world
for the way it really is

hate is a powerful force
to be used against others
but hate is the wildest of fires
when it starts spreading
in you

the silence is louder
than the words you
articulate
a laugh more counterfeit
than the smile you attempt
to portray
and a person so broken
even their heart struggles
to stay awake

i get shamed for what i wear
looked down upon like a second-hand garment
exposing my shoulders
wearing a fitted skirt
means i deserve what's coming next

except
it shouldn't
it was made for me to adore
not to entertain
the desires of others

if you asked me
what does it mean to be a real friend?

i wouldn't know what to say
because no one's ever
been a real friend
to me

no one would ever be able
to hear how i truly feel

because
hearing about the loss
of someone you
loved
would make your heart
stop

between a rose
and a sunflower

why do you always pick the rose?
no matter how many
thorns
get caught in your
veins

nice guys finish last

because
they make sacrifices
for others
to get ahead

we can be of the same blood
same species if it's not satisfactory
but when it comes to
male and female
being female
is never enough

you underestimate me
not because i'm young

but
because you fear
where you'll end up
if i don't choose your path

what's the point
of living
if it's not my life

why is it so hard to
walk away

when they
already left

CHAPTER 2

I'M FINE

it's quite peaceful
being alone
the silence of it all
says everything
i need to hear

there's a difference
when i say that i'm lonely
or when i say i'm alone
being alone is a
physical state
being lonely
isn't

sometimes i wish i were a
butterfly

butterflies are free
when i'm not

people are dangerous
but our minds are even more powerful
words float off our tongues
sharp enough
that even a knife can't dare
to challenge them

physically
they do no harm
but mentally
they wreak all havoc

i was always told
not to be like everyone else
but i see all their
real smiles

and wish i was
just like them

why are we growing up in a world
that loves what we see
but not who we are
one fragment is enough
for the torment to rise
an infamous flood of comments
Something that seems to be normalised

why are we growing up in a world
with standards further than the sun
where beauty only means this or that
and nothing in between
why be in a world
that only scans the surface
when i know that i'm more than
what everybody sees

if i'm underwater
getting pulled into the waves
i won't scream for help
because i've always
fought my battles
alone

i'm too sensitive
i lack courage
she sheds too many tears
she's a complainer
he acts too shy
he's a loner

i'm too sensitive
because of fear
she sheds too many tears
because it's how she feels
he acts too shy
because he's not ready to be seen

some of
the worst pain
is not being there
for the person
that needs you
the most

i did it
out of love
they said

well if that's love
then i don't want it

i'm not your everything
i'm simply just
another
thing

the hardest moment
in a movie
isn't the ending
but it's everything
that happens
in between

people
are like gold
eventually
all the beauty
tarnishes away

the only time they care
is when the thing they
actually love
walks away

i've been in the shadows
even in the spotlight

sometimes
light just makes
it harder to see

parents only seem to
accept one side
of you
so why tell us to
open up
when you only
listen to
half of what
comes out

don't tell me to
just breathe

when you took
my air away

i've learnt to stay silent
because
no one listens
to
a stupid child

the words
i love you
get tossed around
so recklessly
like a deck
of cards
so now i don't know
what to believe

the cards all look
the same
to me

why do others
force upon us
the tasks
they themselves
cannot fulfil

i'm too young
to be this invested

but it's not my fault
that poetry opened
its heart
before you did

why do we
have to drown
before we can
live

if you think
i've never made a life-changing
decision
think again

i traded my happiness
for your
pain

i wish i could
forget you
but sadly
this type of
love can never
disappear

stop playing with me
like a dice on
a board
because
unlike a dice

i'm fragile

don't look at me
with those tragic eyes

i wished for the world
when you tore it down

when i close my eyes
my guard stays up

even in my dreams
i find no peace

i don't waste my breath
asking where you are
when i don't even know
where i am

promises ruin lives just as much as they build them. a promise can be the weightless balloon that lifts you up. but a promise can also be the anchor that trails you down. promises are a hurtful thing. because who ever really keeps them? i don't blame you for not knowing the door you were opening up. you didn't know if you were falling onto silk or rocks. but you chose to push. instead of pull. so i had to swallow the key for that door to never be opened again.

i'm so disappointed
your achievement means
nothing
you sit and
observe
lacking any room
for ambition

i'm so disappointed
you have my blood
in your veins
but you're nothing like
me
and i'll say it again

i'm so disappointed
from parent to
child
try say it again
but watch them
slowly die
inside

you give me everything
except the chance to
live

now i understand
why adults say to cherish
your childhood

and i may be young
but i feel as though my
childhood ended
before it even begun

i sacrifice too much
for others

now i'm left with
nothing

how am i capable
of pleasing everyone
except for myself

when i say
i want to love
i mean from the
novels i read

your anger ruined
the idea of love
so now i don't know
what love is

why can people leave
yet your love for them
is left behind

i waste my energy
on those
that don't even glance
in my
direction

your words are
heavier than the
breaths i take

your petals were full
of life and love
then they wilted
and died
with your
withering lies

- *a severed chance*

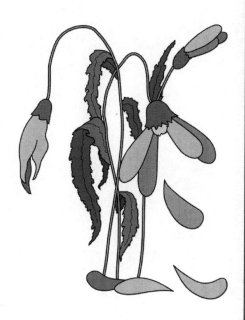

saying goodbye
is the hardest word
i've had to say
when my world was
still yours

leaves fall off the
autumn trees
away from the branches
they used to hold

the way that people
leave the ones they loved
and forget everything that
they used to know

CHAPTER 3

I'M SORRY

i begged for you
you reluctantly asked for me
i yearned for you
you barely ached for me
i needed you
you never wanted me

the word sorry
is so meaningless
yet so significant

the power it holds
depends on the beholder
the pain it can bring
depends on its tone

but could i ever forgive
the words that were said
when they abandoned your lips
without a single regret

ships embark on the
greatest journeys
with only the universe
holding the plans for
its course

in the most
treacherous times
those ships will sink
engulfing every ounce
of life with it

i have come
to terms
that one day
my ships will sink

so i must build
my own
instead of boarding
others

- *the turmoil of friendship*

my heart doesn't
have to be yours
for you to
break it

it's always been
open

and yet no one reads
the word
fragile
decorated on
my broken walls

the scenarios in
my mind
fill the lonely spaces
that reality
pretends to fill

happily ever after
only lives in
the books
i read

because society
doesn't allow
any room for
happy to
be seen

the intensity
of my words across
an isolated page
are the intensity
of the world
shoved into a
shattered vase

but if something
is broken
then the pieces
can't fit
so they'll knead us
into shape
until our cries whisper
i quit

but as they always say
what does a foolish
teenager know about
the intensity
of reality
anyways

i spent so long
hating you
that the memories
of me
loving you
were nowhere
to be found

i make sure others
feel the love
i wish i could
receive

i value those
in my life
more than
myself

because
they're the
stars i look
up to
before i
close my
eyes

the voice
in my head
keeps me
sane...

...without it
i'd have to
endure the
depths of
pure and utter
loneliness...

...even though
i'm already
alone

i will never
be enough

but i can *have*
enough
to satisfy
society's idea
of being
enough

it's easier for
me to hide behind
the words of others

than to take
off my mask
and show them
who i really am

holding back tears
in the darkness of
your room
is like holding back
a tsunami with
the palm of your
hands...

...eventually
you'll break

i think of
scenarios to escape
the sickening poison
of the real world

but when i hear
the warmth in your
voice

suddenly
i don't feel like
i need to
get away

i had felt a
powerful longing
for something before
but this time
it was different

i didn't just want you
i needed you

but as long
as your laugh
heightened with the
tones of the wind
and your smile
wore crescents
in the corner of
your cheeks

i could be happy

when leaves descend
onto the ground

the sound it makes
when stepped on

is how my heart
broke

when i fell for
you

the difference between others and i, is that i've already found my soulmate. not a lover. but a best friend. the one you write letters for. the one singers strum their guitars for. the one who jumps when you jump. and the one who opens their arms when yours are bound to your side. one of the lessons i've learnt in life, is that your soulmate doesn't have to be somebody you're in love with. but it's somebody that teaches you a new type of love. somebody that waits for you on the other side. and somebody that waters the life in your eyes with a single smile.

when i was lost. you found me again. when the bitterness of *sorrow* shackled me in my cage, you set me free. the angered '*i did it because i love you*' became buried under the genuine warmth of your *i miss you's*.

even if we said goodbye, your love still paints with the stars in the sky. and while the earth spins, i'll look through the glass roof. wallowing away in my thoughts, until i find the one with you.

~ *Julianne Littler & Patricia Marciniak*

i was so fixated
on the idea
that i had to
appear happy
through your
eyes

that i
abandoned what
real happiness
was supposed
to resemble
in mine

the voice in my
head has all the power
in the world

but the voice that
really speaks
lacks all the
bravery
to speak
up

it's undemanding
writing a story
with a pen and paper
knowing there can
be a happy
ending

but in life
i'm compelled
to turn the page
even if my
character doesn't
get to meet her
well-timed end

i never thought
the one i needed
to stay

would want
to be a stranger
instead

i crave for the
days where smiles
weren't temporary
veils

i reminisce in the
days
where we wanted
to fast-forward

not
end it all

heartbreak
sounds like the
most penetrating
torture to
endure

you must inevitably feel
that pain
even after it becomes
embedded with the
love of the next
charmer

i say
i don't take things
for granted
but

why do i dwell
on the past
while my future
awaits forgivingly

sometimes
i feel as though
a point
with an explanation
makes the knife
in my back
hurt a little
less

i never regret
the first encounter
with a tender
soul

but i
regret not
leaving the ones
that tried to
ruin me

when i closed my eyes
i used to dream of you

now when i close
my eyes
i'm in a nightmare
obstructed
by you

the second
worst pain i've
felt is when i had
to say goodbye

the first was
the tormenting
intermission

knowing i'd have
to let them go
in the fullness of
time

i must be the villain

not due to
the fact that i
could be a repulsive
individual

but because
people in my life
always seem
to leave

it's never easier
to deceive
than be sincere

you can either
ease their pain

or feel it

why am i dwelling
on the past
rather than living
in the present

long ago
i lost my voice
but you sacrificed yours
so i could be
heard

i don't miss you
but i never
declared
that

i didn't love you

don't insist i'm
nothing

when i gave you my
everything

how long must i
beg for you
to hear me
when you shield
your ears at the sound
of my voice

nothing ever
makes me truly happy

everything is purely
a **distraction**

i feel as though
you turn me into poison

but i await in hopes
that you'll grow
to be my
antidote

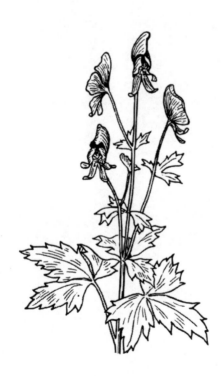

i learnt to forgive
when the person who
wound me
was you

CHAPTER 4

I'M ENOUGH

the stretch marks
that are drawn on my body
aren't marks
of embarrassment

but marks
of my journey

who created
the standards that
us as women
are expected
to be

i had already started
staring blankly
at my figure
my facial features
and who i was

begging
wanting
needing
to replicate those
other girls
because that's what
they all call
beautiful

but beauty
is in the eye
of the beholder

and as the beholder
beauty is all i see

don't let them
into your heart
until they find the key

they may just
block the airways
that let you breathe

stop expecting what
i can't give

and start accepting
what i can

why do you shame others
when even you
aren't the definition
of perfect

we're all simply
bundles of sunflowers
that are waiting
to bloom

don't be afraid
to shut the door

it was only
opened to let
you see
what blinded
you

we let our minds
deceive our hearts

when they did
what they did
and said what
they said

so in the end
you still chose to
believe

your arms
are like ropes

one second
they're bound
around my frame

then the next
they snap
with no more
arms to be
found

why wait until
tomorrow
when tomorrow
may never
come

learning to accept
who you are
is learning to
accept who you aren't

don't let the little
things provoke you

they shape the
bigger things

i have fallen before too
and yet i still
keep going

because
the prize in the end
makes it all
worthwhile

we should all
be broken at
some point in
our lives

so we can
reshape ourselves
into more than
a lump of clay

pencils don't always
draw the perfect
line

like pools of money don't
always make
the perfect
life

don't lose yourself
when you lose someone
else

your fails
may be the
weights holding you
down

but your fears
are the hurricanes
pushing you
back

silence is a label
that binds us
shut

so rip off the label
no matter how much
it hurts

hate and love
don't form a balance
one side always tips
just a little further

don't be
the puppet

be the
puppeteer

learning to be like
everyone else
can be like learning
to ride a bicycle with
no handlebars

- useless and tiring

stop expecting to
find stars
when you look up
at the sky
use your own glow
to find your
path

as you gaze into
the mirror
you're beautiful
nonetheless
but beauty shines
best
when you see
your genuine self
staring back at
you

if i weren't meant
to have these scars

the winds would've
changed its
course

expecting others
to be like you

is asking a
bird to fly
without its wings

- *utterly impossible*

i don't speak
what i feel

just investigate
my eyes

and a story
will be told

listen when i say
don't run away
from your problems

but run away
from the conniving
problems
that aren't yours
to solve

my words are more
alluring than my voice

but my voice is the
pencil that sketches
my words

thank you for
leaving
when i wouldn't

*- pain teaches lessons that
comfort cannot*

our minds and our hearts
ruin us in equally
beautiful ways

why do people crave
to see others fail
just to excuse their
own failures

- *how envious of you*

parents are capable of
making you hate what you
love

the way they're capable of
making you love what you
hate

the sacks under my eyes
don't carry the exhaustion
from lack of sleep
but they carry the fatigue
from lack of happiness

yes. you hurt me but i let you stay. not because i didn't feel the pain but because you were too important for me to say goodbye. letting you go would be like the moon leaving the earth. without the moon there'd be no light in the sky for me to pursue. it would resemble the eternal darkness that i already carry in the arteries of my heart. you carry my heart with unstable hands but i carry yours with the spine of my back.

ABOUT THE AUTHOR

Taryn Kisaalita is a young student born in 2006, whose parents are originally from Uganda but was raised by her mother in North London. Her early interest in the creative arts led her along the path of poetry and in the year of 2016, she participated in a Young Writers Competition. Her acrostic poem *Happiness*, was published in the book *Poetry* Emotions, as well as her second poem in the book *Mum In A Million*.

While the Covid-19 lockdown of 2020 brought suffering, torment, depression and loss, Taryn wrote to depict the feelings of teenagers around the world. The art of writing has followed her for countless years leading up to her much-anticipated publication of *Past 3am* which marks the birth of her new-found journey.

Printed and bound by CPI Group (UK) Ltd, Croydon, CR0 4YY